Understanding the Elements of the Periodic Table™

CARBON

Linda Saucerman

rosen
central™

The Rosen Publishing Group, Inc., New York

To my husband

Published in 2005 by The Rosen Publishing Group, Inc.
29 East 21st Street, New York, NY 10010

First Edition

Library of Congress Cataloging-in-Publication Data

Saucerman, Linda.
Carbon / by Linda Saucerman.—1st ed.
    p. cm.—(Understanding the elements of the periodic table)
Includes bibliographical references and index.
Contents: Fire ignites interest in carbon—Carbon finds a place at the table—Carbon in the natural world—The key to life—Carbon compounds—Carbon goes on a date.
ISBN 1-4042-0155-6 (library binding)
1.   Carbon—Juvenile literature. 2.   Periodic law—Tables—Juvenile literature.
[1. Carbon. 2. Periodic law—Tables.] I. Title. II. Series.
QD181.C1W8 2004
546'.681—dc22

                                                                    2003024427

Manufactured in the United States of America

On the cover: Carbon's square on the periodic table of elements; the atomic structure of a carbon atom (inset)

Contents

Introduction

Hollywood legend Marilyn Monroe said they "are a girl's best friend." But no matter what nickname we give diamonds, they are made of just one single element—carbon.

Along with being beautiful, expensive, and prized, a diamond is one of the hardest known natural substances on earth. It is also one of the oldest things you will ever own. Most natural diamonds are more than 3 billion years old. Diamonds have been around longer than humans have existed on earth.

But carbon (C is its chemical symbol) isn't always as hard as a diamond. Ironically, carbon can also be one of the softest substances known to man. Carbon's softest form is called graphite, which is the "lead" portion of your pencil. Additionally, carbon does not always take the form of a solid.

Carbon can be found in some common gases. When it reacts with oxygen, it can form carbon dioxide (CO_2). This is the scientific name for the gas we release from our bodies every time we exhale.

Most important, carbon is found in every living thing. From dinosaurs to dogs, carbon is a component of all life, both past and present. All forms of life, including numerous things we use every day, owe their existence to a form of carbon.

Chapter One
Fire Ignites Interest in Carbon

Mankind has known of carbon for centuries, but no single person is credited with discovering this element or giving carbon its name. The word "carbon" comes from the Latin word *carbo*, meaning ember or charcoal. Because fire was one of the first things humankind ever knew, fire remnants—soot and charcoal—were very common in the ancient lifestyle and thus were also named carbo. When a natural item that contains carbon, such as wood, is burned, carbon becomes concentrated as soot, charcoal, and ash. Soot, charcoal, and ash are forms of carbon called amorphous carbon, which you'll learn more about in chapter three.

The ancient Greeks first developed the concept of an element. They claimed that everything was made up of at least one of the four elements—earth, air, fire, and water.

In the mid-seventeenth century, British philosopher and chemist Robert Boyle agreed with the idea that there are basic elements that make up everything. But Boyle claimed there were many more than these four elements. Boyle theorized that everything was made up of very small particles of matter. Matter is anything that has mass and takes up space. Boyle concluded that these particles of matter could only be differentiated by their shape and motion. These particles, classified by their differing shapes and motions, became known as elements. Boyle

British philosopher and chemist Robert Boyle developed the theory that everything is made up of matter. In 1660, Boyle helped found the Royal Society of London, the world's oldest scientific society.

is often associated with the identification of carbon as an element. But it would take other scientists, including Englishman Sir Humphry Davy, to show that coal, soot, charcoal, and diamonds were all versions of the same element—carbon. After carbon was identified, scientists later realized that it can be either the hardest or one of the softest substances, depending on its form.

The Anatomy of an Element

To understand how elements behave, you have to think small—really, really small. An element is one of the more than 100 known substances that cannot be separated into simpler substances by physical or chemical means. For example, if you take the element iron (Fe) and melt it down, you cannot turn it into another element. If you hammered a piece of iron, you wouldn't be able to change it into another element.

No two elements are exactly alike, and all elements are made up of atoms. In fact, all elements *are* atoms. Atoms are the basic building blocks of all matter. Atoms unite with other atoms to form a molecule. Different forms of carbon, such as graphite or diamond, are made by different combinations of carbon atoms that make different molecules.

The nucleus of the carbon atom contains six positively charged protons and six neutrons, which have no charge. Surrounding the nucleus are two shells of negatively charged electrons. The first shell contains two electrons, while the second contains four. The carbon atom has room to add four more electrons to its outer shell.

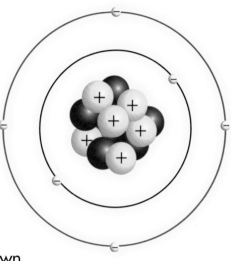

Subatomic Particles

Until the early twentieth century, scientists believed the atom was the smallest structure known to mankind. That was until scientists realized that atoms have structure, too. The main particles that make up atoms are protons, neutrons, and electrons. These are called subatomic particles. Protons have a positive electric charge; neutrons have no charge; and electrons have a negative electric charge. All atoms contain a nucleus, or center, where the protons and neutrons are contained. Outside of the nucleus are shells, or

Carbon has been assigned the chemical symbol "C" on the periodic table. The number in the upper left corner represents the atomic number, or the number of protons the element contains. The number in the upper right corner represents the element's atomic weight.

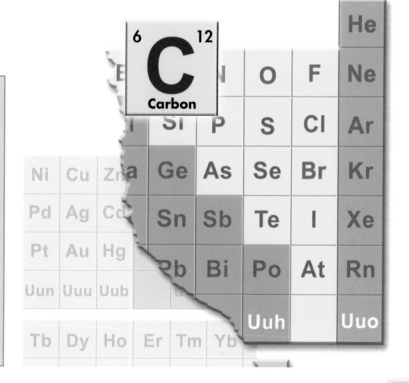

Carbon $^6_{12}$C Snapshot

Chemical Symbol:	C
Properties:	Nonmetal, combustible solid; comes in four allotropes: diamond, graphite, white carbon, buckminsterfullerene
Discovered By:	Not attributed to one person; element has been known of since prehistoric times
Atomic Number:	6
Atomic Weight:	12.011
Protons:	6
Electrons:	6
Neutrons:	6
Density of Solid:	Diamond: 3.5 grams per cubic centimeters; Graphite: 2.2 g/c^3
Melting Point:	3,773 K, 6,332°F, 3,500°C
Boiling Point:	5,100 K, 8,721°F, 4,827°C
Commonly Found:	Everywhere

layers, that contain the electrons. The first shell can only hold two electrons, the second shell can hold up to eight, and the third shell can hold up to eighteen. An atom can have up to seven shells of electrons. A carbon atom has just two shells of electrons.

A certain combination of protons, electrons, and neutrons will create the carbon atom. By examining the atomic makeup of carbon, you'll see that it always has six protons and six electrons. The number of protons and the number of electrons of an element are almost always equal. The number of neutrons can vary depending on the type of carbon atom. The number of protons is called the atomic number. The periodic table is organized according to the atomic number of each element, from the lowest to the highest. Carbon's six protons place it as the sixth element on the periodic table, so it is not a heavy element compared with the more than 100 elements that follow it on the table.

It is the subatomic particles that make carbon, or any element, unique. If we were somehow able to take away a proton from carbon, it would have five protons and then would be a totally different element—boron (B). If we were able to add a proton, giving it seven protons, it

5	11	6	12	7	14
B		**C**		**N**	
Boron		**Carbon**		**Nitrogen**	

One proton makes all the difference. While carbon sits between boron and nitrogen, these elements are drastically different. What separates these three elements is their differing number of protons.

would become another element—nitrogen (N). So the number of protons in the nucleus of an atom determines what element it is.

The makeup of carbon's protons, neutrons, and electrons gives it the ability to bond, or join, very easily with other elements to form compounds. This ability to bond easily is one of the reasons why carbon and carbon compounds are so common in our universe.

There are two main types of bonds that hold carbon compounds together—covalent and ionic. Covalent bonds are created when atoms share electrons. Ionic compounds are made when electrons are given from one atom to another. It's almost like electrons are puzzle pieces—some fit together by one filling another's void and others fit together by locking together.

Another important property of an element is its atomic mass (atomic weight). The atomic mass is approximately the sum of the number of protons and neutrons in the nucleus of the atom. Electrons are very light and do not really factor in to the weight. Carbon's atomic mass is 12.011.

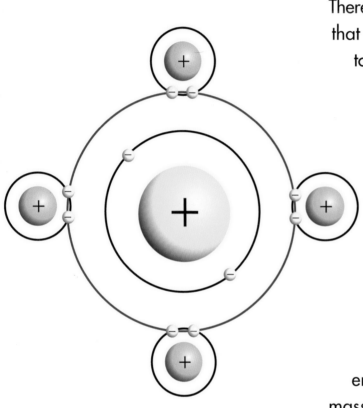

Carbon easily bonds with other elements. The above diagram demonstrates one atom of carbon forming covalent bonds, or sharing electrons, with four hydrogen atoms. The diagram shows the atomic structure of methane (CH_4), an important part of natural gas.

Chapter Two
Carbon Finds a Place at the Table

In 1869, Russian chemist Dmitry Mendeleyev developed the periodic table. As a professor of chemistry at the University of St. Petersburg in Russia, Mendeleyev wanted to create a more organized way for his students to study the elements. He placed the elements in horizontal rows according to their atomic mass, with the lightest in each row on the left and the heaviest on the right. Not all the elements that we know today had been discovered during Mendeleyev's time. However, he did know the weights of hydrogen (the lightest) through uranium (the heaviest known at the time) and arranged them accordingly, placing carbon sixth in the table.

The modern periodic table takes Mendeleyev's idea and makes it a little easier to understand. The periodic table we use today is arranged in horizontal rows called periods. In each period the elements are arranged in the order of their atomic number. The modern periodic table differs from Mendeleyev's original version, which arranged the elements according to their atomic mass. For carbon, though, arranging it by atomic mass or atomic number doesn't make a difference. It is the sixth lightest of all the elements and its atomic number is six as well.

Elements also are arranged in the periodic table by groups. Group numbers appear above each vertical column of the table. There are two main subgroups, A and B, each of which has eight groups. For example, some group numbers are IA, IIA, IB, and IIB. All of the elements within a

Russian chemist Dmitry Mendeleyev devised the periodic table to aid his students. He claimed that the form for the periodic table came to him in a dream.

group have similar chemical properties. These properties affect the way an element reacts during a chemical change (how the atoms are rearranged to make an entirely new substance). These differing chemical properties are sometimes referred to as "families" of elements. The elements in the A groups, such as carbon, are known as representative elements, or elements that add electrons to the outermost shell. Elements in the B group are transition elements, or elements that add electrons to the inner shells of the atom. Transition elements are malleable, conduct electricity and heat, and can form covalent bonds.

Many of the groups have a name. For example, elements in group IVA, where carbon is the first element, are called the carbon group. Carbon is a nonmetallic element, which means that it does not act as a metal. However, the other elements in the carbon group—silicon (Si), germanium (Ge), tin (Sn), lead (Pb), and ununquadium (Uuq)—are not in the nonmetallic family. In fact, from silicon to ununquadium, these elements are a metal in some form. However, all these elements do share some qualities, which is why they are in the same group.

Friendly Electrons

Elements in certain groups have similar chemical behaviors because of their electric forces. If you've ever held two magnets together and felt the

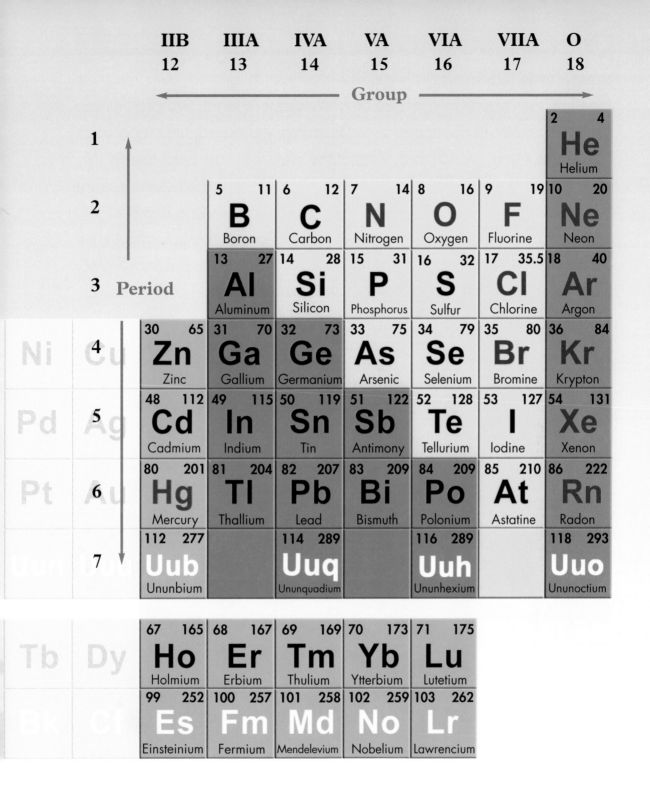

	IIB	IIIA	IVA	VA	VIA	VIIA	O
	12	13	14	15	16	17	18

Group

Period							
1							2 4 **He** Helium
2		5 11 **B** Boron	6 12 **C** Carbon	7 14 **N** Nitrogen	8 16 **O** Oxygen	9 19 **F** Fluorine	10 20 **Ne** Neon
3		13 27 **Al** Aluminum	14 28 **Si** Silicon	15 31 **P** Phosphorus	16 32 **S** Sulfur	17 35.5 **Cl** Chlorine	18 40 **Ar** Argon
4	30 65 **Zn** Zinc	31 70 **Ga** Gallium	32 73 **Ge** Germanium	33 75 **As** Arsenic	34 79 **Se** Selenium	35 80 **Br** Bromine	36 84 **Kr** Krypton
5	48 112 **Cd** Cadmium	49 115 **In** Indium	50 119 **Sn** Tin	51 122 **Sb** Antimony	52 128 **Te** Tellurium	53 127 **I** Iodine	54 131 **Xe** Xenon
6	80 201 **Hg** Mercury	81 204 **Tl** Thallium	82 207 **Pb** Lead	83 209 **Bi** Bismuth	84 209 **Po** Polonium	85 210 **At** Astatine	86 222 **Rn** Radon
7	112 277 **Uub** Ununbium		114 289 **Uuq** Ununquadium		116 289 **Uuh** Ununhexium		118 293 **Uuo** Ununoctium

67 165 **Ho** Holmium	68 167 **Er** Erbium	69 169 **Tm** Thulium	70 173 **Yb** Ytterbium	71 175 **Lu** Lutetium
99 252 **Es** Einsteinium	100 257 **Fm** Fermium	101 258 **Md** Mendelevium	102 259 **No** Nobelium	103 262 **Lr** Lawrencium

The structure of the periodic table has many purposes. You can tell a lot about an element just by where it sits on the table. Carbon sits in group IVA, also known as the carbon group. From carbon down to ununquadium, the elements in the carbon group change from nonmetallic to metallic.

strong force that makes it impossible for you to stick the two magnets together, then you have an idea of what happens when two protons are near each other. Because protons are positively charged, they repel each other. Neutrons, which are electrically neutral, can help lessen this repulsion between protons. But it is the negatively charged electrons that really determine how elements behave and react with one another.

In a carbon atom, four of its six electrons are in the outermost shell of the atom and are known as valence electrons. These valence electrons are very "friendly," as they allow carbon to form covalent bonds. Covalent bonds result when two atoms share a pair of electrons. For instance, the air we exhale from our lungs is carbon dioxide (CO_2)—

Carbon can be extracted from ordinary table sugar ($C_{12}H_{22}O_{11}$) by the process of dehydration. First, sulfuric acid (H_2SO_4) is poured into a jar containing sugar (1). The acid then reacts with the sugar (2), removing the hydrogen and oxygen, which escape as gases to produce smoke and a smell of burnt sugar (3). The carbon remains and begins to expand (4).

Uut and Uup Get on the Table

In January 2004, a team of American and Russian scientists announced the creation of two new superheavy elements. Both elements will fill in gaps at the lower end of the periodic table. Element 113 is named Ununtrium (Uut); element 115 is named Ununpentium (Uup). The new elements are called superheavies because of their enormous atomic mass. However, Uut and Uup will not be given a permanent place on the table until other laboratories have confirmed the existence of the two new elements.

Carbon's outermost shell contains valence electrons that readily bond with other elements to form covalent bonds. This illustration shows the covalent bonds in CO_2, or carbon dioxide.

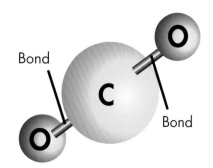

the combination of one carbon atom and two oxygen atoms. In addition to bonding with other elements, these valence electrons allow carbon to bond with itself to create other substances like diamonds and graphite.

The final element found in the carbon group is one of the last to be discovered. Ununquadium was reported in 1999 by scientists in Russia who were experimenting with various isotopes. An isotope is an atom that has the same number of protons as usual but a different number of neutrons. Ununquadium has only been developed in the laboratory and has never been found in nature. It has yet to be determined if it is really a single element. Ununquadium is also extremely radioactive and dangerous.

Chapter Three
Carbon in the Natural World

We know that diamonds, charcoal, and the graphite in our pencils are all made of carbon—these are considered allotropes of carbon. Allotropes are the physical forms an element can take. Valence electrons are what make allotropes possible. You learned in chapter one that electrons are found in shells orbiting the nucleus. Of the two shells in a carbon atom, the outer shell (valence shell) can hold up to eight electrons. Carbon's valence shell has four electrons. This means that each carbon atom has room in its outer shell for four additional electrons. These four additional electrons can be from other carbon atoms or from atoms of other elements.

Diamonds

In diamonds, each carbon atom shares all four of its outer electrons with other carbon atoms through a series of bonds. These bonds form the diamond's unit cell, which is the unit repeated to form a crystal. A crystal is a molecule that takes on a shape according to a repeating structure of unit cells. The tightness between the atoms in the crystals contributes to a diamond's hardness. It is also why diamonds have such a high melting point—6,332°F (3,500°C)!

The arrangement of the crystals also determines a diamond's shape. An octahedron, an eight-sided figure, is the most common shape

This model demonstrates the tight bonds between carbon atoms to make a diamond. The bonds between these atoms are so tight that a diamond is one of the strongest substances known to man. The bonds between atoms create unit cells. The unit cells are then repeated to form the diamond's crystal.

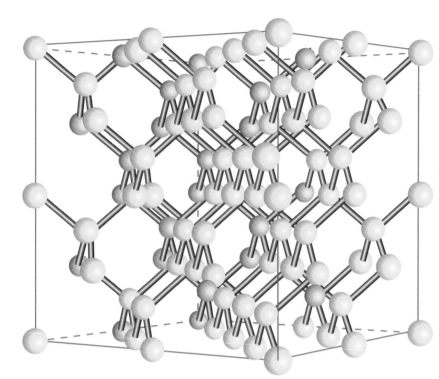

for a diamond. A diamond can also take on other shapes, depending on how the bonds are repeated.

The tight bonds and density of diamonds give a clue to their origins. In order to create a diamond, carbon atoms have to be squeezed together under an enormous amount of pressure. According to the American Museum of Natural History, the pressure needed to make a diamond is the equivalent of turning the Eiffel Tower in Paris upside down and balancing its spire on a five-inch (thirteen-centimeter) plate.

Naturally occurring diamonds are created deep in the earth, in an area called the mantle, where heat and pressure are intense. Diamonds are common in South Africa, where they can be found in ancient volcanoes, in riverbeds, and on the ocean floor. Diamonds are also found in Australia, Brazil, Canada, and Russia, among other countries. Microscopic diamonds have also been found in some meteorites. Natural diamonds can be completely clear, cloudy, or a variety of colors, ranging from pink and purple to yellow.

Natural diamonds take millions of years to be created. These diamonds can be very precious. The diamond pictured above sold for $4.25 million in 2003. Diamonds can also be made by artificial means. However, these diamonds do not have the same value as natural diamonds. Artificial diamonds are commonly used in the construction industry to cut stone.

Graphite

On the other end of the spectrum is another form of carbon, called graphite. Graphite is a form of carbon that is dark in color, has a layered structure, and is very soft. Unlike those in a diamond, the carbon bonds of graphite are very loose. The loose bonds allow graphite to move very easily and create a substance with a hexagonal (six-sided) crystal shape. When graphite is used in a pencil, its loose bonds break apart, easily transferring onto a piece of paper as you write.

In the 1950s, scientists discovered how to make diamonds out of graphite by applying very high pressure and temperature to the

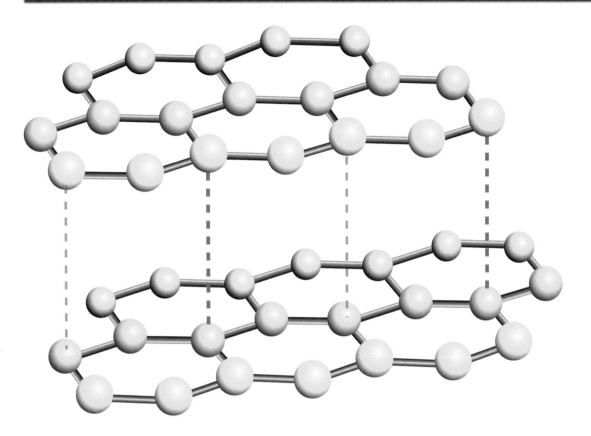

This model demonstrates the loose bonds between carbon atoms that form graphite. These loose bonds allow graphite to break apart easily.

substance. Within a few hours, such conditions force the bonds of graphite to become very tight, much like a natural diamond. However, scientists can't change a diamond into graphite.

Artificial diamonds aren't sought after like the naturally occurring gems. But science has improved artificial diamonds so much that it is difficult for people to tell the difference between a natural and a man-made stone.

Many synthetic diamonds are used as tools. These diamonds have the same hardness as natural diamonds, but they can be made very large and are used to cut concrete and bricks and to drill deep into the earth.

In its natural form, graphite is a gray, soft substance similar to charcoal; it is a common form of the element carbon. Because of the loose bonds in graphite, it is perfect for use in pencils. When you write, the bonds holding the graphite together actually break apart, leaving behind graphite as pencil marks.

Like natural diamonds, synthetic diamonds have an extremely high rate of thermal conductivity. This means that a tremendous amount of heat can pass through the diamond without damaging it. Because of this, synthetic diamonds are being explored for use as semiconductors, which are materials used to transmit electricity.

White Carbon

Another allotrope of carbon is called white carbon. It was discovered in 1969 when graphite was subjected to high temperatures and little white crystals appeared. Not much is known about white carbon, and scientists are still considering whether it is a true allotrope.

Buckyballs

In 1985, a fourth allotrope of carbon was discovered. Buckminsterfullerene (C_{60}) was produced when two scientists zapped graphite with laser beams. The carbon that was formed had molecules that looked like the design of a soccer ball. The scientists named the new allotrope after the American engineer R. Buckminster Fuller, who designed dome houses that resembled soccer balls. The long name of the allotrope was soon shortened to the nickname buckyballs. Buckyballs are still being studied and explored for use as semiconductors.

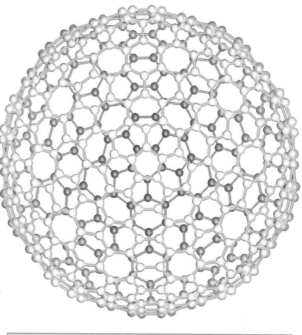

In 1985, a team of American and British scientists discovered buckminsterfullerene. Since then, several other fullerenes have been identified. A fullerene is a closed hollow carbon compound with pentagonal (five-sided) and hexagonal (six-sided) faces.

Amorphous

Amorphous carbon is another form of carbon. However, it is not an allotrope because it is not an elemental, or pure, form of carbon. "Amorphous" means that it doesn't have a definite shape or form. In the case of amorphous carbon, carbon can take many different crystal shapes. It is often in a powder form and sometimes contains other elements. Examples of amorphous carbon are found in charcoal, coal, peat, and soot. Whenever you use charcoal during a barbecue, you are cooking with amorphous carbon.

Coke is a nearly pure form of amorphous carbon and is made by heating coal in the absence of air. The fire from heating coke will burn hotter than a wood fire and has been used to recover iron from ore, the natural mineral from which the metal is extracted. Many amorphous

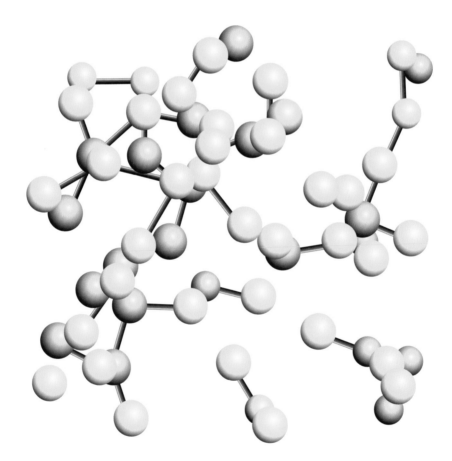

Unlike graphite or diamonds, amorphous carbon has no definite crystal shape. Examples of amorphous carbon can be found in charcoal, soot, and coal. Amorphous carbon is found in fossil fuels, which can be burned to create energy.

forms of carbon are fossil fuels such as coal, oil, or natural gas, which can be burned to create heat or power.

Death and Diamonds

Since diamonds are pure carbon and people are made out of carbon, can diamonds be made out of people? They sure can. In fact, a company outside of Chicago will even make diamonds out of your dearly departed dog.

When a person or animal dies and the body is cremated (burned to ashes), a machine can be used to extract the carbon from the remains and turn it into graphite. The graphite is placed in a vice that exerts 1.6 million pounds of pressure per square inch. After this immense pressure is applied, the graphite is then cooked to 3,500°F (1,927°C). The whole extracting, squeezing, and heating process takes about four months before the graphite turns into a diamond. The process takes a little longer if you want a really big diamond. One woman's ashes were used to create a large diamond that now hangs in a window as a decoration.

These diamonds are not flawless like some of the diamonds found naturally, but they are pretty and come in a variety of colors, including blue, yellow, and red. The cost to create diamonds from ashes starts at around $2,000 for a ¼-carat diamond. It is estimated that there is enough carbon in the ashes of a human corpse to create fifty small diamonds.

Chapter Four
The Key to Life

In the beginning of this book, you learned that carbon is the main ingredient for life. You, your teacher, your dog, the trees in the park, the birds in the trees, the worms in the soil—all of these living creatures contain carbon. In fact, there are about 4 ounces (113 grams) of carbon for every pound (0.45 kg) in a human being. So if you weigh 100 pounds (43 kg), you contain about 20 pounds (9.1 kg) of carbon. With carbon making up more than 20 percent of our bodies, it makes sense that carbon is called one of the building blocks of life. Other building blocks include hydrogen, oxygen, nitrogen, sulfur, and phosphorus—all of which combine easily with carbon.

But it is carbon's ability to bond with itself that really holds the key to life. When carbon atoms join together, they create chains that are either branching or straight. These chains serve as the foundation for other elements to latch on to and ultimately create an enormous number of chemical combinations. Deoxyribonucleic acid (DNA) is one of these chains. DNA is found in every single cell within plants and animals, and it can copy itself. DNA is the molecular makeup found in every living thing—it determines who (or what) you are. DNA determines your hair color, your eye color, your skin color, how tall you are, if you have dimples . . . it is the recipe for you!

Detective DNA

Inside all forms of life, from a housefly to a hippopotamus, is DNA. Carbon plays a role in DNA as a carbon sugar, called deoxyribose, which helps construct the long chains of DNA. These chains of DNA are found inside the cells of every living thing. The cell is the smallest unit of living matter that can exist by itself. These cells are a tiny mass of protoplasm surrounded by a cell wall (in most plants) or a cell membrane (in most animals). Most cells contain a nucleus, much like an atom does. Inside of the nucleus are chromosomes, which are the structures that bear the genes, or the characteristics of heredity. It is the different combinations of DNA within these genes that create different people.

DNA has become very important in solving crimes. Except for identical twins, no two people have the exact same DNA, and DNA cannot be altered in any way. When a serious crime is committed, police detectives are careful to look over the crime scene and collect anything that may later be used as evidence. Blood, hair, skin, saliva, and other pieces of genetic evidence are often found at crime scenes. The DNA contained in those samples can provide the information necessary to crack a case.

Organic Chemistry

Knowing that carbon can readily combine with other elements to create DNA, let's take a look at other combinations, or compounds. Compounds can be made up of just two atoms, such as the simple formula of one carbon atom and one oxygen atom (O) to create carbon monoxide (CO). Or carbon compounds can be made up of several atoms, such as chloroform ($CHCl_3$), which is one atom of carbon, one

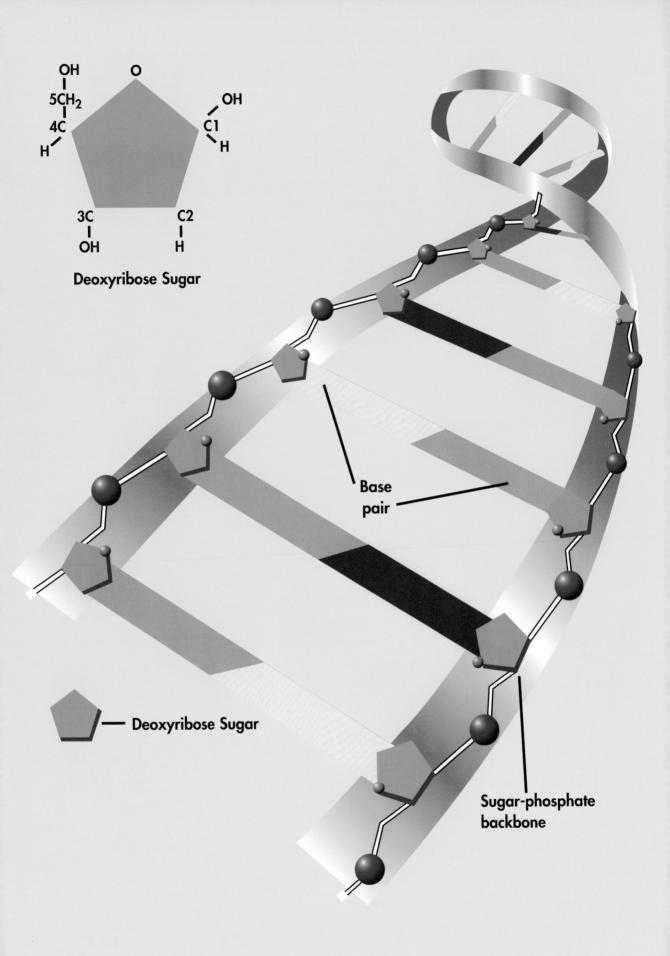

OH
5CH₂
4C
O
H
3C
OH
C1
OH
H
C2
H

Deoxyribose Sugar

Base pair

Deoxyribose Sugar

Sugar-phosphate backbone

atom of hydrogen, and three atoms of chlorine (Cl). Compounds can even be made up of hundreds of atoms, such as carbon fluoride ($C_{60}F_{60}$), which is made up of sixty atoms of carbon and sixty atoms of fluorine (F). Because so many elements can interact with carbon, the field of organic chemistry has been developed to study carbon and its compounds. It is called organic chemistry because it is the study of organic compounds, which all contain carbon.

Carbon Cycle

One common carbon compound is carbon dioxide (CO_2), and it is something that we are all constantly creating. Every time we breathe in, we inhale oxygen (O_2). This oxygen fuels our bodies and is then converted into carbon dioxide, which we exhale. This process is the very beginning of what is called the carbon cycle. There are two parts to the carbon cycle, the carbohydrate cycle and the protein cycle.

The first part of the carbon cycle is the carbohydrate portion. The first step in this cycle is the absorption of this carbon dioxide by plants as part of photosynthesis. Photosynthesis is when a plant absorbs carbon dioxide from the air, combines it with the water (H_2O) it receives from its roots, and transforms it into oxygen (O_2), sugar ($C_6H_{12}O_6$), and starch. Starch is mainly sugar molecules strung together. Any of these sugars or starches found in foods, especially in plants like potatoes and wheat, are carbohydrates. Because pastas and breads come from plants like wheat, these foods also contain carbohydrates. Carbohydrates give us energy. When you eat pasta, you are consuming carbohydrates.

So, how do animals absorb these starches and sugars? Well, for the same reason that you have carbohydrates in you—you eat them. When

Carbon is crucial to the makeup of deoxyribonucleic acid (DNA). Each unit of DNA contains a five-carbon sugar called deoxyribose. These sugars act as the backbone for DNA. The base pairs hold genetic information to decide who or what you are.

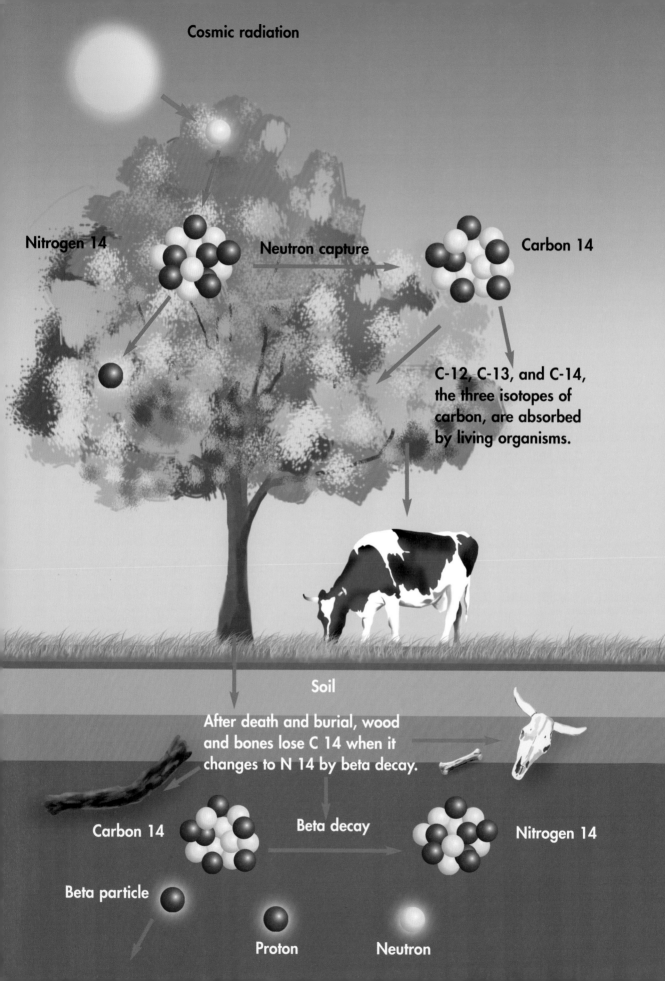

Cosmic radiation

Nitrogen 14

Neutron capture

Carbon 14

C-12, C-13, and C-14, the three isotopes of carbon, are absorbed by living organisms.

Soil

After death and burial, wood and bones lose C 14 when it changes to N 14 by beta decay.

Carbon 14

Beta decay

Nitrogen 14

Beta particle

Proton

Neutron

a cow eats grass, it is absorbing carbohydrates from the blades of grass. Then the carbon cycle begins anew.

Your body transforms these carbohydrates into energy to keep your heart pumping and your lungs breathing. When you exhale, this carbon dioxide is absorbed by a plant for photosynthesis, and the cycle begins again.

But there is also the protein portion of the carbon cycle. What is different in this cycle is that one of the final portions of it occurs when an animal or plant dies. When you are living, you go through life eating carbohydrates and exhaling carbon dioxide. But when you die, your body decays and releases carbon. The carbon from your body marks the end of the protein portion of the carbon cycle and the beginning of a new one. The carbon from any dead plant or animal, including humans, will feed the soil that will help plants grow.

Over a long, long time, your decomposed body and the carbon and other elements it releases will be squeezed under enormous amounts of pressure from the earth's crust as it shifts and changes. Like the bodies of dinosaurs, when you die, your body will eventually become fossil fuels. This marks the end of another aspect of the protein-carbon cycle. These fossil fuels will be burned, and the release of carbon dioxide and other carbon compounds from the heat is the beginning of another carbon cycle.

Every living (and dead) thing plays a role in the carbon cycle. The carbon atom that starts out in a plant can travel to an animal and is released back into the atmosphere either through exhalation of carbon dioxide or through decomposition. This carbon atom could then be reabsorbed by the same plant and start the cycle all over again. Carbon atoms are the ultimate recyclers.

The carbon cycle *(opposite)* begins in the air as carbon dioxide (CO_2) and is absorbed by plants. The plants are then eaten by consumer animals, such as cows, that absorb the carbon. The carbon is then returned to the air during exhalation in the form of carbon dioxide. It can also reenter the air after the animal dies and the carcass begins to decay.

Throughout this book, we have learned that carbon is one of the most common elements on earth. Its ability to bond with other elements to create compounds gives the sense that carbon is everywhere . . . and it is! Let's take a look at some other common carbon compounds.

Hydrocarbons

Along with fueling our bodies with carbohydrates, carbon and hydrogen can also team up to provide the energy that runs our cars and provides electricity for our homes. These chemical compounds are called hydrocarbons. There are a number of different molecular combinations of hydrogen and carbon. For instance, methane is a hydrocarbon, and its formula is CH_4. Propane, another hydrocarbon, is C_3H_8. Hydrocarbons are found in petroleum, natural gas, and coal. When you ride in a car, a bus, or an airplane, you are experiencing the energy of carbon. As combustion or heat is applied to the gas, it breaks apart the hydrocarbon molecules. This causes energy to be released in order to power the car, the bus, or the plane.

One of the drawbacks of using fossil fuels is that there is a limited quantity of them. Fossil fuels are literally made from fossils and take millions of years to be converted from ancient animal and plant matter into

Carbon in dry ice (frozen CO_2) sets off a reaction that is used throughout the entertainment industry to give the effect of fog. A chunk of dry ice can be placed in water (1), and the water will begin to bubble. The extreme cold of the dry ice melts in the warm water (2), which produces water vapor mixed with gaseous carbon dioxide (3).

fuel. Some experts estimate that there is only enough fossil fuel to last us until the year 2040. If we want to continue to travel as freely as we do now with our automobiles, trains, and airplanes and if we want to have electricity, we have to find a new power source other than fossil fuels.

Carbon and Pollution

Another downside of burning fossil fuels for energy is that they release pollutants. Carbon dioxide, carbon monoxide (CO), and

While carbon is one of the most useful elements, it can also be one of the most harmful. This photograph is of pollution lingering over the Bay of Bengal in India.

cyanide (CN) are just a few of the pollutants that are expelled from the exhaust pipes of automobiles and other vehicles that run on fossil fuels. Carbon dioxide has been called a "greenhouse gas." This is because, like the glass panes of a greenhouse, carbon dioxide will allow solar radiation into the earth's atmosphere but it will not let it out. The amount of carbon dioxide and other greenhouse gases being released into the atmosphere has increased greatly ever since the invention of the automobile and other similar machines. The increase of greenhouse gases has been attributed to global warming, which has caused massive polar ice caps to show signs of melting. Greenhouse gases and the greenhouse effect also have been linked to smog, a hole in the ozone layer, and other major environmental concerns. To combat these problems, governments worldwide are encouraging industries and scientists to explore other fuel sources, such as solar energy, wind power, and water power. Some carmakers are developing cars that run on hydrogen and create virtually no pollution. These alternative cars are starting to gain popularity, with celebrities such as Cameron Diaz and Leonardo DiCaprio buying and driving them.

Deadly Carbon Monoxide

In addition to pollutants being released by cars and other vehicles, some carbon compounds, especially carbon monoxide, can be a serious threat to your health—and carbon monoxide can be found right inside your home! Carbon monoxide is expelled by home furnaces, kitchen stoves and ovens, and water heaters that burn fossil fuels. When these appliances are working properly, carbon monoxide and other harmful fumes are released through vents outside of the home. But if these appliances are malfunctioning, carbon monoxide can seep into the air inside the house and become deadly to its occupants. In fact, more than 200 people in the United States are killed each year by home appliances leaking carbon monoxide. Because carbon monoxide is invisible, odorless, tasteless, and does not make any sound when it is released from a leaky pipe, it has been called a silent killer. Fortunately, inexpensive carbon monoxide detectors can be purchased at almost any hardware store to prevent carbon monoxide poisoning.

Plastic and Pollution

Fossil fuels are also used to create plastic. If you stop and look around, you'll see that plastic is used for a lot of different things. From cups to pens, plastic is very multifunctional. One of the good things about using plastic is that it will not break like glass, and it is very lightweight.

Plastic is very useful, but it is also very difficult to decompose in a landfill, the final resting place for our garbage. It can take up to twenty years for one plastic fork to begin showing signs of decay. So one little piece of plastic really can add to our growing landfills. Using fossil fuels

It all piles up. Landfills, like the one pictured, help control pollution. But some carbon-based pollutants, such as plastic, take too long to decompose, therefore taking up too much room in landfills. Plastics recycling has helped reduce the problem of overcrowded landfills.

to create plastics is not the best way to use our depleting natural resources, and it also isn't environmentally responsible. Many fast-food restaurants are now using plates and sandwich containers made from paper. This paper is made from the renewable resource of trees and will decompose faster in a landfill than plastic will.

Other Carbon Compounds

In addition to the numerous carbon-hydrogen combinations, there is almost a never-ending amount of other carbon-based compounds.

Pour Yourself a Glass of Carbon

Every time you have a sip of soda, you are drinking carbon. In 1767, Joseph Priestley of England was experimenting with carbon dioxide gas and realized that it could be dissolved in water, creating a fantastic dance of bubbles. This concoction tickled the tongue, and seltzer water (also called soda water) became quite popular. Nearly 120 years later, a pharmacist in Atlanta, Georgia, created a concoction of coca leaves, kola nuts, and carbonation, and Coca-Cola was born. Today, this brown bubbly beverage and others like it are made mostly of water, caramel syrup, and carbon dioxide.

Here's how they make a two-liter bottle of soda: The syrups and water are mixed in a bottle, and carbon dioxide is added so that it fills up the remaining space in the bottle. Then the bottle is quickly capped. As soon as you open the bottle, you hear a hissing sound, which is the release of the carbon dioxide from the bottle. The more carbon dioxide that escapes, the faster the soda will go flat. When you pour yourself a glass of soda, the bubbling of the soda is caused by carbon dioxide being released into the air.

Look up the word "carb" in the dictionary and check out all the words that follow it. You'll see that from the word "carbachol" to the word "carburize," and nearly all of those words in between are related to carbon in some way.

Calcium Carbonate

When the element calcium combines with carbon, it creates a chalky substance called calcium carbonate ($CaCO_3$). This substance is mined

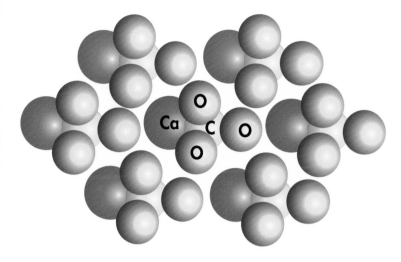

Calcium carbonate ($CaCO_3$) is one of the most common carbon compounds. It can be found in chalk, plaster, pearls, cement, and cosmetics. Calcium carbonate is also one of the Earth's most common minerals.

in mountains, but it is also present in seashells and animal and human bones. Calcium carbonate is a big part of the art world because it is found often as a white chalk. As a part of paint, it can be mixed with other colors to blend and lighten hues. The chalk that you write with on the blackboard at school is also made of calcium carbonate, as is the plaster in the walls of your home.

Besides paint, chalk, and plaster, calcium carbonate can also be used as a medicine to cure indigestion. Nearly every antacid you see in the pharmacy contains calcium carbonate. When your stomach is upset and churning with gastric acids, the calcium carbonate from one of these tablets will absorb and neutralize the acids and calm a stomachache. Another benefit of taking calcium carbonate is that it contains calcium, an element and mineral that promotes healthy bones and healthy bodies.

Chapter Six
Carbon Goes on a Date

In addition to being able to readily combine with other elements, carbon also has a number of isotopes. An isotope of an element is an atom that has the same number of protons but a different number of neutrons. Carbon has several known isotopes, which have two to fourteen neutrons in the nucleus. Each of these isotopes is very interesting, and scientists have found a special purpose for nearly each one.

Carbon 14 is a naturally occurring radioactive isotope with a half-life of 5,730 years. This means that it will take 5,730 years for half of this element to decay. Besides being present in nature, carbon 14 can be made artificially in a nuclear reactor. Carbon 14 is present in every organic thing because it combines with oxygen to form CO_2 and then becomes part of the carbon cycle. Not all CO_2 compounds contain carbon 14, but they may contain one of the thirteen other isotopes of carbon.

The great thing about carbon 14 is its use in archaeology, in a process called carbon dating. Through the food we eat and our daily existence on earth, we are constantly taking in carbon 14. Nearly everything alive is constantly absorbing carbon 14. But when you die, you stop absorbing carbon 14, so the present amount in your body slowly begins to decay. Archaeologists can guess the age of a fossil by how much carbon 14 is found in the specimen.

Carbon 14, shown here, has eight neutrons and six protons in its nucleus. This isotope of carbon is used in carbon dating. Carbon 14 exists in nearly every living thing. By analyzing the amount of carbon 14 found in a specimen, scientists can estimate the age of that specimen.

So, when a scientist measures the amount of carbon 14 present in a fossil, he or she compares it with a plant or animal in its present-day form. For example, scientists can compare the amount of carbon 14 in a fossilized fern leaf with the amount of carbon 14 in a modern fern leaf. From this scientists can estimate when the fossilized fern died by figuring out when it stopped producing carbon 14.

So let's say you are studying to be an archaeologist and are digging at what is believed to be a site where ancient people once dwelled. While you are digging, you come across two bones that look to be from an animal, possibly a deer. To determine if these bones came from a deer that had been dead for a few years or for thousands of years, you will take it back to the lab and measure the carbon 14 levels in each bone. The carbon 14 levels are really high in one of the bones. In fact, it is the same amount of carbon 14 as the levels in a deer that is only a few days old. Meanwhile, the other bone you found has very low levels of carbon 14. This bone has levels consistent with other bones that have been determined to be from

The process of carbon dating begins in the atmosphere when cosmic ray protons blast nuclei, which produce neutrons. These neutrons then bombard nitrogen, a main ingredient of the Earth's atmosphere. This reaction creates the isotope carbon 14, which combines with oxygen to form carbon dioxide. The carbon dioxide is then incorporated into the carbon cycle, where it is found in nearly everything—living or dead.

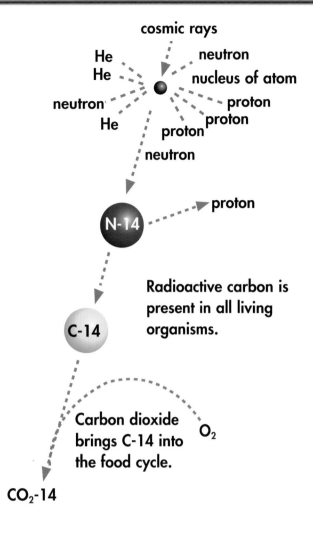

Radioactive carbon is present in all living organisms.

Carbon dioxide brings C-14 into the food cycle.

the year 1200. Knowing this, you can estimate that the first bone you found is from a recently deceased deer, and the second bone is from a deer more than 800 years old.

The Name Game

There are a lot of factors that go into naming a carbon compound: the type of bonds it has; whether it has a cyclic structure (the atoms are arranged in a ring); and if the compound includes hydrogen. One way scientists keep track of all this is by using prefixes to identify how many carbon atoms are in the compound. "Methyl" describes a carbon compound with one carbon atom; an "ethyl" compound has two carbon atoms; "propyl" has three carbon atoms; "butyl" compounds have four carbon atoms; "penta-" has five carbon atoms; and "hexa-" has

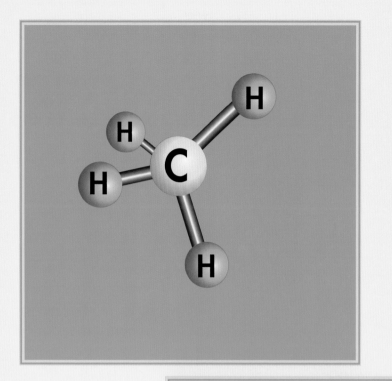

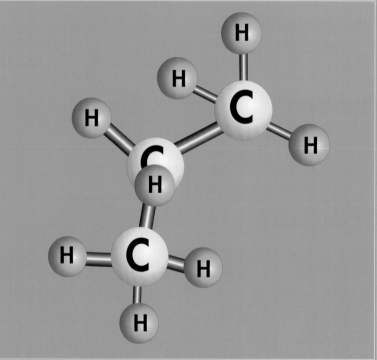

The structure and bonds of carbon compounds can help name the compound. The top model is the molecular structure of methane (CH_4). "Methyl" is a prefix that describes a carbon compound with one carbon atom. The bottom model is the molecular structure of propane (C_3H_8), which has the prefix "propyl," meaning the molecule has three carbon atoms.

six carbon atoms. For example, methane (CH$_4$), a flammable and gaseous hydrocarbon commonly found in natural gas, is one carbon atom bonded to four hydrogen atoms. Ethane (C$_2$H$_6$) is a colorless, odorless gaseous hydrocarbon that is also found in natural gas and used as a fuel.

Carbon compounds are also named after their bonds. An alkane is a single-bonded hydrocarbon; an alkene is double bonded; and a triple bond is an alkyne. Methane is an example of an alkane. To learn about other carbon compounds, simply open up a dictionary and look up words that begin with methyl, ethyl, propyl, and butyl.

Carbon is a highly versatile element that can be found everywhere. It can be as hard as a diamond and

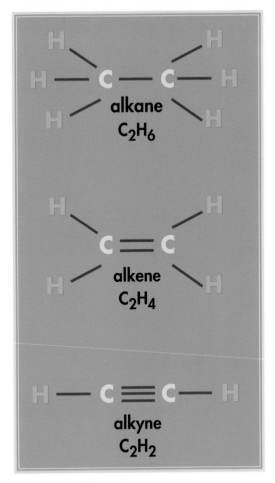

Hydrocarbons are classified by their different bonds. Alkane, alkene, and alkyne are found in different types of fuel resources.

as brittle as embers. It can be clear as crystal or black as coal. From a single match to a garden of daisies to plastic soda bottles, nearly everything contains carbon. The carbon cycle is going on every second, every minute, every hour, and every day, and you are a part of this fantastic cycle of life.

The Periodic Table of Elements

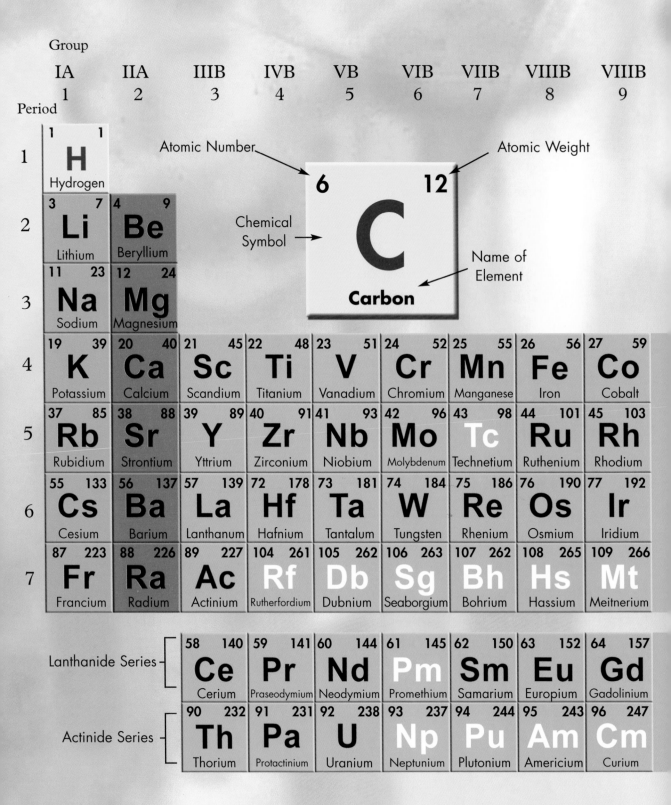

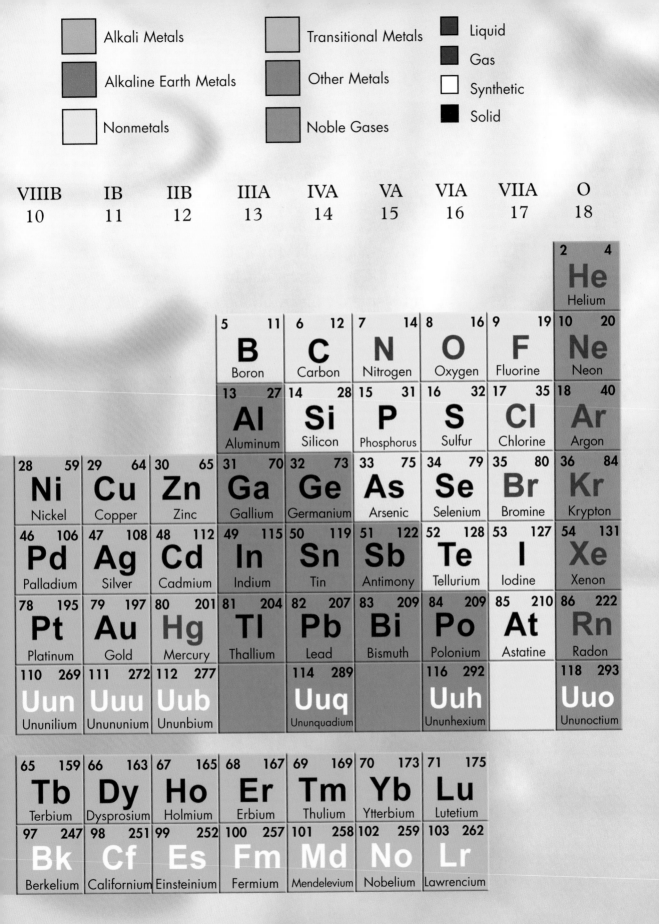

Glossary

atom   The smallest, most basic unit of an element. Atoms can exist alone or in combinations.

atomic mass   The mass, or weight, of one atom of an element.

atomic number   The number of protons in the nucleus of an atom, which is equal to the number of electrons. The atomic number determines an element's place on the periodic table.

combustion   The act of burning; a chemical process that produces heat and light.

decomposition   The act of breaking down into simpler parts or elements.

electron   A negatively charged particle found outside of the nucleus of an atom.

element   The basic matter that all things are made of. Any substance made of one kind of atom.

group   The elements that are in a column of the periodic table.

molecule   The smallest particle of a substance.

neutron   A particle within the nucleus of an atom that contains no charge.

nucleus   The positively charged central portion of an atom.

period   A horizontal row in the periodic table.

proton   A positively charged particle within the nucleus of an atom. The number of protons and electrons are almost always equal in an atom.

protoplasm   The living matter in cells that contains carbon, hydrogen, oxygen, nitrogen, sulfur, and phosphorus.

American Museum of Natural History
Central Park West at 79th Street
New York, NY 10024-5192
(212) 769-5000
Web site: http://www.amnh.org

Los Alamos National Laboratory
PO Box 1663
Los Alamos, NM 87545
(505) 667-7000

Web Sites

Due to the changing nature of Internet links, the Rosen Publishing Group, Inc., has developed an online list of Web sites related to the subject of this book. This site is updated regularly. Please use this link to access the list:

http://www.rosenlinks.com/uept/carb

For Further Reading

Gardner, Robert. *Kitchen Chemistry: Science Experiments to Do at Home*. New York: Julian Messner, 1989.

Strathern, Paul. *Mendeleyev's Dream: The Quest for the Elements*. New York: St. Martin's Press, 2001.

Stwertka, Albert. *A Guide to the Elements*. 2nd ed. New York: Oxford University Press, 2002.

VanCleave, Janice. *Janice VanCleave's Chemistry for Every Kid: 101 Easy Experiments That Really Work*. New York: John Wiley and Sons, Inc., 1989.

Bibliography

American Museum of Natural History. "Where Does the Carbon Come From?" Retrieved August 2003 (http://www.amnh.org/exhibitions/diamonds/carbon.html).

Arizona State University. "Ask a Biologist." Retrieved August 2003 (http://askabiologist.asu.edu).

Los Alamos National Laboratory. "Periodic Table." Retrieved August 2003 (http://www.lanl.gov).

Stwertka, Albert. *A Guide to the Elements*. 2nd ed. New York: Oxford University Press, 2002.

WebElements Ltd. "Carbon." Retrieved September 2003 (http://www.webelements.com/webelements/elements/text/C/key.html).

Weisstein, Eric W. Eric Weisstein's World of Biography Web site. Retrieved August 2003 (http://scienceworld.wolfram.com).

Index

About the Author

Linda Saucerman is an editor and writer living in Brooklyn, New York, with her husband and their dog and cat.

Special thanks to Rosemarie Alken and the Westtown School, Westtown, Pennsylvania.

Photo Credits

Cover, pp. 1, 7, 9, 10, 13, 15, 17, 19, 22, 26, 28, 36, 38, 39, 40, 41, 42–43 by Tahara Hasan; p. 6 © Bettmann/Corbis; p. 12 © SPL/ Photo Researchers, Inc.; pp. 15, 31 by Maura McConnell; p. 18 © AP/Wide World Photos; p. 20 by Cindy Reiman; p. 20 (inset) © Lester V. Bergman/Corbis; p. 21 © Clive Freeman/Biosym Technologies/Photo Researchers, Inc.; p. 32 © NASA/Photo Researchers, Inc.; p. 34 © Francesc Muntada/Corbis.

Designer: Tahara Hasan; **Editor:** Charles Hofer